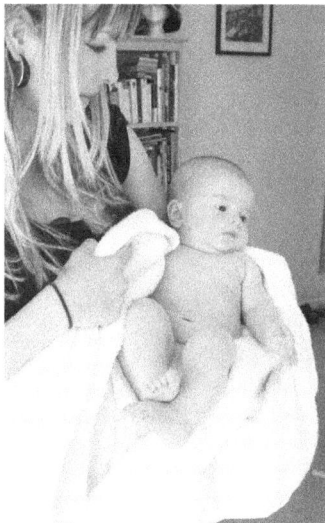

One of the strongest human desires in life is—
the desire to have children.

Elysse

FERTILITY GODDESS SOVATA

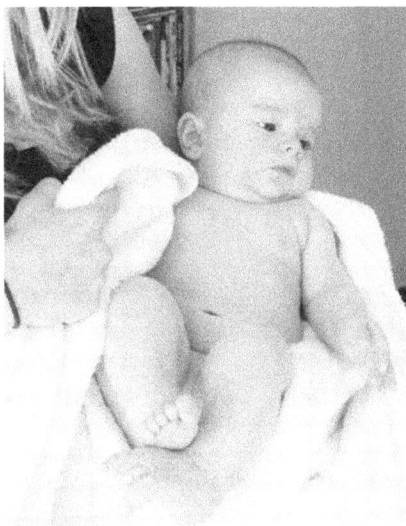

BY
Elysse™
POETIS

FERTILITY GODDESS SOVATA©

by Elysse Poetis™

EDITOR
Elizabeth A. Jordao

Copyright & Intellectual/Creative Property of the author/poetess, Elysse Poetis™
starting with © 2010 and beyond.

This first original published in 2010 by
VON DER ALPS PUBLISHING CORPORATION
www.vonderalps.com
CANADA

www.elyssepoetis.com

CANADIAN CATALOGUING IN PUBLICATION DATA

ISBN 978-0-9782302-5-8

Printed in USA

TABLE OF CONTENTS

CONTENT: PAGE:

CHAPTER ONE

CHAPTER TWO

CHAPTER THREE

Book dedicated to
globals who desire to:

travel
have fun
live healthy
procreate
nurture
inspire

Elysse

Chapter One

STORKS

EVERYWHERE

Why?

I t was 28 years since I left Transylvania—in 1998 when I travelled back there simply as a companion to my 81 year old mother who had a health scare and insisted that I travel with her immediately, to see her daughter (my sister), and her brothers and sisters. I realized in the end that her desire to go was largely directed towards the place she called home for the first 55 years of her life, before she came to Canada.

From Toronto, as we embarked on the Austrian Airline, we both had become a bit emotional—I probably more than my mother.

For me, in 1980 when I left, it was almost clear that I might never go back to Romania.

In those days my life was in danger, and in fact the danger stayed with me for the next two decades. Anyway, I can tell you that my mother does not understand much of what I went through—the dangers I faced, the secrets, the refugee camp, the hunger while pregnant, the fear, threats, etc. To her, those things happen to an extreme only in the bible, in fiction, in movies, and to other people. Apropos, she does not distinguish reality from fiction when it comes to parts of the bible. Numerous times I struggle to explain to her, but in an instant she would get upset—very upset. Then she would take me for a biblical ride all the way to Egypt, Moses, Jerusalem, Jesus the savior, or those nasty Romans, and, of course, the villain of all history, the Devil itself. Often she would dress the conversation with apocalyptic predictions of her own, making my experiences look pale in comparison. I could never compete with my mother's imagination. I ask myself, "Why didn't she learn English properly? She would have been a bestseller in fiction, for sure."

No need for me to further mention to you any of the spicy conversations with my mother all the way to Vienna. At the arrival over the sky of Europe, she looked at me a bit surprised when my eyes were flooded with tears. The memories came back like a flashlight in my eye. Flying over the very Alps I so much love ... Over the heads of so many people who helped me ... Over countries that protected me from ending up dead—the remembrance was just too emotional.

Once in Vienna, a few hours later we embarked on Tarom, the Romanian Airline, and flew to Cluj, a very large Transylvanian city famous for arts, universities, beautiful people and its historical grace. A long time ago, in German language Cluj was called Klausenburg. It was built by Germans as a fortress to protect Transylvania from invaders who were coming and going totally uninvited. Historically, Europe did not have it easy, but due to the courage of so many europeans, that continent made it! First, through permanent small wars—then through the biggest world wars humanity have ever experienced! Europeans distance themselves from the tribal cultures that they inherited from their ancestors, and forcefully, step by step, modernize themselves. Look at them now! Healthy, inspiring, elegant, kind, very educated, and wealthy.

Civilization springs out of people's courage to change—we learned over and over again.

The Romanian airline, Tarom, has daily flights to Vienna. How convenient! Everything was good. My mother was excited. I was happy to see her happy, and on top of all that good, Gina, my cousin who is a head nurse at a pediatrics hospital in Bistrita, along with her brother Mihai, came to pick us up. They surprised their mother, who is my mom's sister, by bringing her along. Adriana, my nice, who is a student in economics (in Bucharest), was driving, because Mihai, her father, had an accident—something hit him right in the eye and could not drive. These people, except for Gina, drove all the way from the city of Roman, Moldova, just to surprise us. On the airport they come with flowers. When my mother and her sister came face to face—oh, my God! The laughs, the tears, emotion all around. My mother put her purse down and ran to embrace her sister. I had to be vigilant, look after her purse (passport), because she behaved like a kid.

Enough with our arrival. I'll move on. As we drove from Cluj towards Bistrita, we passed through many communities. It was so peaceful to just watch. These cities, towns, and villages, had one thing in common:

STORKS!

My question? Why would these storks go back to the same place every spring after spending the winter in a tropical warm place? Why the attraction? Why do they choose the same tree? Actually I should mention that they build their nests so big, with straw and mud—and, God forbid!— no one would dare to ruin them. The storks nests stay like that forever! They are sacred! Generation after generation these big birds use the same nest to have children.

You should see how they carry snakes to their babies ... Sometimes a large frog is being airlifted by one leg, helplessly hanging in there, kicking and screaming in mid air all the way to the altar. The same with fish, mice, and large insects. Even small baby animals. These storks eat meat! Like humans! I'm sure they eat other things also, like veggies, fruit, cereals, seeds.

Observing and observing, left and right,

while back in the passenger seat squashed between my 81 year old mother and her 79 year old sister, what really surprised me was the fact that so many things have changed. In a way I felt alien to Transylvania. It felt like I was in a dream. After 28 years in the Western World, my entire being has changed. From the first moments of my journey it was clear to me how much I have changed—that I see things differently, in great detail, and with great compassion. Besides, it is only natural since maturity grounded me good.

Actually, before landing in Cluj I was looking from above, focusing on the infrastructure. Sincerely, I wish I had a magic wand to upgrade some things.

All my life I felt the need to help, to promote, and to create good and beauty—and I pray to God for such abilities every day of my life.

My love for life and creation hurts me.

When I do good I feel better. But now, let me tell you that what I discovered while looking out the window from my cousin's car, impressed me! People were elegant and seemed calm. Some were walking for pleasure with their fancy puppies, others working around their properties. It was clean. It was peaceful. It felt safe.

The energies of fear from the '80s weren't there anymore.

The evil was gone.

I could see that people and the local governments have united in common causes and concepts. Parks looked good. The storks that build their nests in dangerous places, like telegraph posts for example, now had a man-made iron basket designed specifically as a base for their nests. I could not believe it! This takes creativity and great compassion towards these big birds. "*I was born in a good country,*" I thought.

From history to modern times, storks are

being perceived to be messengers of fertility, and in Transylvania people feel emotion around this sensible subject. How angelic!

Myself, as a child, I believed that a stork had delivered me to my mother. To this day I prefer to believe just that.

It is so romantic to be airlifted from heavens, by a stork, and landed in the arms of a human family by whom you are being desired. What a beautiful concept! Superior fiction—bestseller in the children's land.

We are talking fertility economics here, being backed up by miracles, and all sorts of folkloric fairy tales. ... and the clever stork right in middle of all miracles! Today, I would not be surprised if the stork made it on the face of collectable stamps. They are everywhere anyway: on greeting cards, party balloons, television programs, movie animation, etc.

Never through eternity will I ever forget the fun I had as a child, watching the baby storks learning how to fly—not to mention the emotions they gave me when they were losing their balance. I lived 19 years in North Transylvania and I witnessed only one tragedy. Back then, those images were like Disney animation for children, only that it was all real—and I'm happy to have discovered that it is still real today. Transylvania is gifted with beauty.

FEW WORDS TO MEMORIZE:

Copil = Child
Copii = Children
Copilarie = Childhood
Copulat = Copulation
Mama = Mama
Father = Tata
Stork =Barza
Nest = Cuib
Puppy = Catel
Cat = Pisica
Horse = Cal
Cow = Vaca

CUCKOO

THE BIRD

Cuckoo!

S torks are intriguing, but Cuckoo with its uttering sound/song/greeting "cuckoo! cuckoo!" is totally outstanding! The forests of North Transylvania are totally charmed by this feathery summer guest and the echo of his "cuckoo! cuckoo!" travelling across the Carpathians. These vibrations of his/her "cuckoo!" travel from mountain to mountain all over. Let me tell you that everyone who was born in Europe, as a child fell in love with Cuckoo.

Canada and United States do not have a Cuckoo. Some scientists/naturalists had imported birds from other places. I'm not going there—telling what kind of birds they did import, considering the annoyance they created in the end by doing so. Some of these birds are so loud and bad musicians that you want to cry if you listen to them for two minutes—not to mention the fact that they multiply like rabbits and create constant discomfort, covering everyone else's voice in the birdy world, with their loud and false notes. Besides, they are quite big and have extra vocal volume. Speaking of nature's performing arts, if you lived in the country side, like I did for a while, you will understand what I'm talking about.

You end up preferring the coyotes' serenades during mating season over the choirs of these loud birds with false voices. They are not forest idols, "like Cuckoo," by any stretch.

Sincerely, I think that these birds are meant for a far away large jungle (from where they must originate to begin with) simply because they greatly disturb all smaller birds—every day snooping in their nests, stealing their food, scaring tiny chicks. That's what I witnessed! Often, I ended up protecting the little ones by chasing the intruders away.

My biggest question to naturalists is, "Why didn't any one ever succeed in bringing Cuckoo here in North America?"

Why? Why not? Did someone try? Was there a tragedy? Is it impossible? Can it be tried again? I'm brewing an idea momentarily ... Aha! I got it! We need a National Geographic team along with Chris Angel, and the Green Party of Canada and US "experts." Experience, magic, and hope, mixed together in a delicate recipe, could work miracles!

Let's be serious now. Did you know that this bird does not need a partner in order to raise children.

Whoever the lucky charmer is, as soon as the egg is fecundated, he is off the hook! No demands. No bird pressure.

Mademoiselle Cuckoolina lays her eggs in other birds nests, confusing many species, often small birds, who wake up to monstrous size chicks, only to end up raising them as their own. ... and Miss Cuckoolina is keeping vigil, observing every move, as her children are being looked after, growing nicely under her creative spying eye, until they fly away singing, "cuckoo! cuckoo!" all the way to liberty—and later, the females repeating what mommy did throughout history. Letting others raise their chicks! It is very interesting to see how these birds behave. Total aliens, independent from the rules of others. Fascinating!

An old saying was circulating in Transylvania, comparing men who impregnated other than their own wife, to Cuckoo.

Why not let the other man love and raise his child/children? And there was no shortage of such cases. If DNA testing would have been possible ... Ha! How many of them would have surfaced. But again, in some cases it was a secret deal. Many couples in desperation, created the possibility and kept it secret.

Speculation, conspiracy theories, it didn't matter.

They loved their kids and that was it!

Some were wealthy and loving couples, and they were crying at the sight of a child.

It is horrible, I know, not to have children when you have this deep love ready for distribution/investment.

Now, I'll leave the Cuckoo story alone, and move on to the another sector, a serious one—infertility treatment at a very famous resort right there in the middle of Transylvania. But before I do that, I'll mention a few more things:

In regards to my trip to Transylvania in the spring of 2008, in the beginning it was sunny—then eight days it rained non-stop—then sunny again! So beautiful ...

It was spring. The trees were flowering. The air was like mint. So very fresh. I could not believe it! Years away from those mountains did temporarily erase some feelings.

From my sisters window, in her living room, every morning I admired the Carpathians, the snow at their top brightened by the Sun rise.

It looked like gold ... Like fire ...

The hills were covered in plantations, all in bloom ... The smell of spring was overwhelming ... Bees and bugs marathonning everywhere. The valleys carpeted in a multitude of green tones. In front of my sister's house was one of those telegraph poles with a couple of glorious storks at its top, in a specially supported nest as I mentioned prior. Every once in a while the storks would leave the nest, fly away, then come back, let their heads arch backwards, and greet each other in a sign of success, welcome, or something of that nature. I suspected that they were preparing to have children. Transylvanian baby storks. Imagine that!

One day as I was sitting peacefully in front of the open window, suddenly, right there under my nose, the Cuckoo came up in a tree close by to greet me. It serenaded me for a while, then took off. I was pleasantly shocked. A few days later I visited an aunt in the next village, and I received very similar treatment from another Cuckoo bird. It was almost like they knew how long ago I left, and how much I missed these sweet childhood memories. Even my sister and my aunt were surprised. Cuckoo never gets so close to houses. *"It is because of me,"* I joked. They didn't laugh. *"This is because of you,"* they said.

Refreshing moments. Little miracles ... For a brief moment I was a child again. I could close my eyes and let those moments freeze the time around me ... But back home, in Canada, I have love! Love that I raised in my own nest! ... and that love produced more love! Besides, now I also have the love of my dreams, my beautiful husband ...

"My beautiful garden of love,

my Canada ..."

And so, my short trip to Transylvania ended soon. When we arrived back in Toronto I was very tired. Not my mother! She was so rejuvenated, so full of energy that she started cleaning her apartment, arranging her flowers, and writing her mail. I could not believe it!

Give the seniors a trip back to their childhood, then just step back and observe.

I could safely argue that they become younger and happier instantly. That's the type of wonderland they desire, we might as well give it to them.

For sure I lost some opportunity during

that time because I was right in the middle of my book tour when my mother seduced me to escort her overseas. Regardless of my initial discomfort, in the end I appreciated the revival of so many beautiful childhood memories. Every such opportunity can trigger fresh ideas, creative ideas. Writers like me need change of sceneries, and Transylvania is more than just that to me. It is the nest I was born in. The land I fed on until the age of 26, when I left for the Western World.

In fact, after a year in Germany and Austria, where Cuckoo was present, I embarked for Canada, a paradise decorated with its own glorious beauty. Canadian beauty, famous around the world.

The greatest part of my development took place here in Canada where the opportunities to learn were infinite. All my life I admired journalists and their communication skills. As a child I dreamed of being able to communicate properly. Canada gave me just that and much more ... the English language. Oh, how happy I am! Thanks to my adoptive mother, Canada, now I can communicate at the global level.

Romanian language is also a romantic language of the world. It is the closest descendant of the Latin language. Elegant and by now totally absorbed in the modern English vocabulary. For me it is an enormous plus. Playing with words is fun, and these two languages combined make my life as a writer so much easier. It is delightful!

Science, philosophy, medicine, theology, etc., are all based/translated from the Latin language. Just read some of the Romanian words and see the common sense:

FEW WORDS TO MEMORIZE:
Man (Human) = Om
People = Oameni
Woman = Femeie (Lady = Doamna)
Man = Barbat (Gentleman = Domn)

Tooth = Dinte
Dental = Dental
Dentist = Dentist
Hand = Mina
Manual = Manual
Finger = Deget
Digital = Digital
Forehead = Frunte
Frontal = Frontal
Good Morning = Buna Dimineata
Good Day = Buna Ziua
Good Evening = Buna Seara
Good Night = Noapte Buna
Good Bye = La Revedere
Hotel = Hotel
Doctor = Doctor
Pregnant = Gravida
Positive = Pozitiv
Negative = Negativ
Good/OK= Bine/Da
I Love You = Te Iubesc
Bride = Mireasa
Groom = Mire
Marriage = Casatorie
Ring = Inel

Cosmetics = Cosmetice
Mirror = Oglinda
Food = Mincare
Wine = Vin
Sleep = Dorm
Sleepy = Somn
Allergy = Alergie
Heart = Inima
Lung = Plamin
Stomach = Stomac
Spleen = Splina
Appendix = Apendicita
Rheumatic = Reumatic
Hospital = Spital
Ambulance = Ambulanta (or Salvare)
Emergency = Urgenta
Help = Ajutor
Thank you = Multumesc (or Mercy)
Menu = Meniu
Water = Apa
Beer = Bere
Wine = Vin
Coffee = Cafea
Ice Cream = Inghetata

Chapter Two

INFERTILITY
CURED IN

Sovata

S ovata is being declared a phenomena in Europe, a woman's paradise, especially if the woman is a sterile one who cannot conceive children without help. The medical help, I should say, can be part of it—but Sovata, the resort itself, is the biggest doctor on the planet.

This God given gift to humanity had turned enormous amounts of childless women into very happy mothers.

Located in middle of Transylvania, Sovata is a resort like no other. Its musical spirit is a classical lullaby played for parents to be. Its choirs are the voices of children wanting to hold the hands of all those who want to conceive. Their giggles are ready to infect the quiet atmospheres in childless homes around the world.

SOVATA ...

The Mother of Fertility
The Goddess of Joy

This unique beauty is dressed in glorious forests, washed by the clean river, Tirnava Mica (Small Tirnava), warmed by lakes with miraculous properties. The five lakes are: Lake Ursu (Bear), Lake Alunis (Chestnut Bush), Lake Negru (Black), Lake Rosu (Red), Lake Verde (Green).

In Lake Ursu (Bear), the salin water is warm (with temperatures rising towards the bottom of the lake). The natural cure factors are: the sodic-chlorinated water, sapropelic mud, especially in the Lake Negru (Black), helio-therapy on the shores of all five lakes, and relaxing protective climate with fresh air rich in aerosols.

Therapeutic procedures used:

- Salt and thermal water bath (all natural) in bath tubs or in lakes.

- Warm mud applications, including intravaginal ones.

- Kineto-therapy.

- Electro and hydro-therapy.

- Helio-therapy.

Sovata is open all year around. Every season has its magic and its benefits. It is a perfect holiday destination for everyone, not only women. Gynecologically speaking, women have declared Sovata a feminine paradise.

Therapeutic recommendations:

Sterility; Ovarian deficiency; Cervicites; Metroannexites; Degenerative (spondyloses);

Inflammatory, abarticular and post traumatic rheumatic affections; Peripheral neurological affections (slight paresis, poliomyelitis after effects), and much more in terms of benefits—not to mention the fun/adventure. We all know, when we cure the discomfort in one place, all other pains and aches are history. Often just stress or loneliness can distort our well being. I know ...

Remember, Sovata, the resort, has its own hotels, treatment facilities, villas, private houses that can be rented, camping sites, e.g. Dealul Ciresului (Cherry Hill). There are also plenty of restaurants, libraries, churches, bars, clubs, etc. Entertainment and trips to the nearby City of Tirgu Mures with a population just under 200,000—and so much more.

Single ladies, keep in mind, please—there are plenty of single gentlemen, some of them permanent frecventees of Sovata. I suppose that their greatest desire is to impregnate the future in the most natural environment. Organic concept, huh? There was a very popular saying in Transylvania, "Take me mommy to Sovata to meet my tata." ... and in Romanian language it rhymes perfectly. **Tata** *means* **Father**.

Bucuresti—Ateneul Roman

Transylvanian students—folcloric dancers from the region of Bistrita-Nasaud, where I grew up.

OTHER FAMOUS RESORTS

IN

Romania

B onus for you—a few famous health resorts in Romania, for cure or simply for fun. Enjoy the discovery and take advantage of the opportunity if suitable.

Famous Resorts for numerous cures:

- **Baile Herculane**—for rheumatic, neurologic and metabolic diseases—a very beautiful place. Very romantic. I've been there as a visitor for fun multiple times, and I loved it.

- **Baile Felix**—24,000 years of thermal water springs. Felix is famous for curing rheumatic, neurologic, and gynecological diseases. In the '70s, I nearly lost my life in Felix. I accidentally slid into one of those gigantic warm pools and I did not know how to swim. Three men jumped in the water and saved me. I visited Felix many more times anyways. It was incredible fun and very elegant.

Baile Herculane—Neptun Pavilion

Along the banks of this river are trails taking tourists towards the caves in the mountains, one of them being named Grota Haiducilor. The crystal clear river can be admired from the restaurants.

Baile Herculane

1. Hercules Complex 2. The Train station 3. The statue of Hercules 4. The park. 5. Hotel Hercules.

Hotel Roman, Hotel Diana, the treatment facilities, the city centre, entertainment districts, etc. — years ago were very attractive.

- Covasna—for cardio-vascular diseases ... and lots of activity for everyone.

- Vatra Dornei—also for cardio-vascular diseases. I visited Vatra Dornei in 1979. It mesmerized me. Great people. Great fun.

- **Buzias**—for cardio-vascular diseases, and fun for everyone else travelling along. These resorts are equipped to entertain families and to cure the family members or friends that need treatment. None of these resorts are plain. Elegance and excitement is everywhere. So much to enjoy. So much to see and learn. I recall an instance when I visited Moneasa (mentioned on the next page) for the first time. While I was enjoying the tranquility, there was a middle aged tourist from Bucharest who said to me:

"What is this jungle? I can't believe this wilderness!"

"What's your problem?" I thought. For sure this man was missing the traffic, the noise, and the fumes of the city. Silly! Always remember that there are people on our planet who would die of heart failure in a quiet clean place. Somehow, they are designed to enjoy the noisiest places, where traffic never stops. In my case, I do enjoy the city, but I enjoy the peace of the country much more. I love listening to nature. I love the clean air, small rivers, mountains, forests, wild flowers, etc.

 - Tusnad, Sinaia, Moneasa, Geoagiu-Bai— for asthenic neuroses. ... and for fun. It is very quiet. Very calm. Like I said, I've been to Moneasa, twice. The best fish I ever ate was in a restaurant in Moneasa. The second time I was there for the celebration of my graduation from Liceul Pedagogic, Arad. We were a group of approximately 30 people, students and professors. Again, it was incredible fun, elegant peace, good food ...

 - Calimanesti-Caciulata—available treatment for affections of the locomotor and digestive apparatuses. This was Napoleon the Third's preferred destination, I learned. I've never been there, but I'll go one day. I'm curious what Napoleon the Third had experienced/liked. Just brushing shoulders with some energy traces of historical power, alone, can be therapeutic to my mind. I believe in transcendence ... In miracles ...

- Slanic Moldova, Singeorz-Bai, Baile Olanesti—for digestive and/or nutrition diseases, relaxation, meditation, etc.

- Eforie Nord, Eforie Sud, Neptun, Mangalia—for locomotor affections and peripheral nervous system diseases. These four famous cities, stars, or satellites, of the Black Sea are balneary resorts unique in Europe. Very, very, popular.

When I lived in Germany, a business man told me that these places are his favourite. He and his wife took their twin small children there every year to make them healthy, to help them develop properly.

I believe it! I've been there, everywhere, and I loved it! It was magic. In Eforie North, the most important balneary resort at the Black Sea littoral, I indulged in mud bathing for two weeks, and I cured myself completely of acute ovarian pain, which prior,

Eforie Sud, fun and elegance at the Black Sea

Olimp, another satellite wonder at the Black Sea

City of Arad, Romania—The Palace of Culture

Arad, Romania—The Theatre

was so severe that it landed me in the hospital and kept me there for a few weeks. ... I was so young ...

Lake Techerghiol was very salty. People did not need to know how to swim in order to float on those waters. It also had some red tiny water creatures, microscopic flower-like organisms that had the property to cure people from rheumatic pain, ovarian pain, too much perspiration, and toxins, etc. In my first book, *The Mind of a Poetess* a true contemporary story, published in 2006, there is a picture of me from that time in 1974 at the Black Sea with my nice, three year old Lily, on page 211.

In my experience, the self treatment was super fun in the open. By booking a vacation there, I shot two rabbits with one bullet—having fun and healing myself at the same time.

The images of hundreds of nude people strolling around, all covered in mud, appeared to me very similar to some pictures of characters straight out of science-fiction (animation movies). Even in those times there were the mother and child fenced in gardens. The same for men; a separate section.

Many mothers from all over Europe brought their children to cure them from over perspiring every night. It worked so nicely even for my three year old nice, which I personally took there for treatment, since I needed it myself. Later she became Miss Arad.

If in 1974 my vacation there was so beautiful and helpful, I can only imagine today. If I had the time and/or opportunity, I would go again in a flash! In fact, I know that I will go back one day to enjoy, relax, admire, eat fish, have a cold drink ...

My suggestion? Goggle the places! See picture. Info in detail. Up to date services. I'm sure you can find an eternity of good, up to date helpful information.

When I write like this, I feel that many would assume that I get paid to promote. No, I do not. I haven't been to the Black Sea in 36 years, but I feel that it is my responsibility as a citizen of this planet to promote the good on Earth that I've discovered, and to let others know what helped me in my despair. Believe me, my life was a rollercoaster out of control until I reached the age of 47—from Europe all the way to America. That's when I decided enough was enough. But that's another story, actually written in 2001, my 432 page memoir book called "The Mind of a Poetess" (by Elysse Poetis, of course)—see: www.amazon.com (available also on Kindle). So many details are in that book that cannot be repeated.

Apropos, I was a sterile, also. I suffered from primary infantility—my genital apparatus stopped developing when I was nine years old.

It took a lot of treatment to bring me to an acceptable development.

I was seventeen when I was forced in an inappropriate bond (called marriage), without personal or parental consent (which according to the law was illegal). Soon after, when I started bleeding severely and experience total discomfort and immense pain (from the unwanted activity), I cried to my aunt Elena who was a head nurse in the city. She had some gynecologist doctors as friends, and took me under her wing for immediate treatment. To force me to develop, these doctors injected me with progesterone and estrogen. Then they injected me with sintofolin to provoke palpitations of the uterus. Sintofolin, which was used to provoke abortions, gave me severe bleeding. To stop the bleeding, the doctors creatively injected me with vitamin K.

When my reproductive apparatus started developing, it upgraded me to the level of a twelve year old girl. Excellent! Successful treatment. The bleeding stopped—but I was sterile and remained so until one day.

Years later, I did get pregnant for the first time, after a cancer operation at the age of 20 (melanoma on my knee)—I think it was because of the treatment and shock. In those days, cancer was perceived to be contagious. People would run from you if they knew that you had cancer. I was hospitalized and put in isolation at The Dermatology Hospital, where I couldn't even have visitors. Eight dying women were in my room, and a little boy with leukemia, only 4 years old.

Going back to the pregnancy, yes I did get pregnant, but that baby was killed in me (at three months), when a gynecologist, Dr Copil, prescribed me a progesterone double dose, arguing that I wasn't pregnant—that I only had a disturbance in my period. Of course, I myself was confused, especially because I did suffer from irregular periods (amenorrhea). This dramatic episode happened to me after I moved to Arad, where I worked full time and was a full time student at Liceul de Arte/Pedagogic. From so much work and activity I barely had time to breathe, never mind menstruate.

During my third month of pregnancy, when I was injected with progesterone double dose—oh, my God, how I nearly died ... I ended up in a coma. It wasn't the first time for me to be in a coma or declared dead, but it was the first time that a baby was killed in me.

The baby died and I didn't.

Trauma is an easy word comparing to what I felt. So stricken I was by grief that I wanted to die. Besides my drama, I also experienced in that hospital some of the most dramatic, cruel realities in the memory of my existence (in regards to abortions).

Those images inflicted in me severe rage and the instinct to fight for women's rights, indefinitely.

Being strong was not enough in those days.
Dictatorship is evil! No one cares!

They want what they want—and that is it!

I cried every day after getting out of the hospital. For the next five years I could not get rid of the grief. Regardless, somehow I had the strength of an elephant, the memory of a super-computer, the energy of an olympian, and the stubbornness of a mule. After a while, I also changed my thinking—and nothing could divert my attention from the brilliant future that I had in mind.

Yes, I suffered—but I also fought. Besides, I had great values! Born with them on board. I had a healthy attitude. No one could de-route me from the smart reality I chose to follow.

Looking back I feel very proud of my mental abilities, my accomplishments, my good spirit ... I'm also very satisfied to know that, even though young, I managed to travel a lot while there. I even did "The Tour of

Romania" by train, first class. Girls of my age were after red nails and silly mini-skirts. In my case, my nails were natural. My mini-skirts weren't so mini (except for one). Bars and disco's did nothing to attract me. I definitely disliked alcohol, smoking, promiscuity, laziness, and gossip. What I did like was good language, books, museums, classical movies, a variety of good music, wise people twice my age, children, and pets. And yes, I loved cinema, movie stars, royalty, and fairy tales. In fact, I felt like royalty all my life.

Cathedrals were also on my list of favourites.

The largest cathedrals were open to the public to go in, pray in peace, and light a candle.

What I really loved in those days, at list between 1973 and 1976, was the fact that many leaders in the city of Arad did not listen to the communist dictators and follow exactly what they recommended. In Arad, at one point, the entire local government was changed overnight—without elections (without people's consent).

Tragedy again, soon after—I had lost five colleagues within two years, all young.

One of them was my mentor. His name was **Ladislaw Brutö**, a 37 year old charming economist, a graduate from University of Economics (Cluj), and a former university soccer player, who died of brain cancer within five months from discovery. This man was loved beyond belief by everyone who knew him. So elegant and beautiful. He was a carbon copy of Christopher Plummer in the movie "The Sound of Music." He's wife, Veronica, did not have children (she married his best friend three months after his death).

Mr. Brutö was like a big brother to me. In fact, he called me "little sister." He was my angel from God, continuously pushing me towards education. Hundreds of times he would check on me and drive me to school himself, making me promise over and over again that I will pursue education all the way. He was devastated when I had cancer and all other times that I nearly died. Also, I realized that he did not mind putting any-one in place in order to protect me. Oh, how I respected him. The grief I suffered when I lost him ...

Another close friend, **David Munteanu**, was shot by the secret service while he attempted to escape Romania, in the waters of the Black Sea. He was only 23 years old, an excellent swimmer. He looked like the statue of King David, a perfect blond with royal blue eyes and golden curly hair. Beautiful young man. His brother was a poet. At the funeral, his sister cried and asked if anyone knew anything about David's endeavours prior to his death.

Being the only one knowing everything he had planned and why, I just sat there quiet

with the secret service focussed on me.

To this day I wish I could tell. If she is alive, David's sister will hear from me one day. I'll never forget the double aluminum coffin he was locked in. The grief of his parents. The traumatized girlfriend …

Dorina was another friend of mine who was a student nurse, with two little boys and her young husband in the army. While he was home for a few days, awarded for his extraordinary performance, Dorina got pregnant. Shortly after he went back, Dorina self-induced an abortion which landed her in the hospital. The secret service at the time was very present in the hospitals. They barricaded the doctors from administering her antibiotics, letting her die of infection. Dorina was 23 years old, the most beautiful young lady you can imagine—loved to the limits by everyone.

Ilonka, was a young Hungarian lady, a friend. A brain aneurism killed her instantly at the fragile age of only 28 (as she bent to fix the corner of the tablecloth). She left behind two very young children and a devastated husband who adored her.

From work, another lady friend, 55 years old, died very fast of advanced cervical cancer (while entering menopause).

You see, I'm older than that right now, but I feel very young. We have changed!

We do not age the same anymore.

Today, I feel very young. Of course, much wiser—and I do not apologize for this God given gift which I worked so hard for all these years. Going back to the dramatic stories, I can only tell you that due to the intensity of my grief, at one point I lost so much weight that I looked like a skeleton—yet, I did not fall apart.

These were just a few examples from my portfolio of suffering.

Many more are in my memoir.

Everyone has its own pain. We all need peace and quiet at times. We need treatment when necessary. We need each other for inspiration. We need sincere love. If you read this book, please, I encourage you to stay positive. Fight whatever is trying to conquer you. Do not give up on love and light. Do not abandon hope.

In 1980, at the age 27, I remained pregnant for the second time. I believe it was due to shock, emotion and fear, in the Austrian Alps, while in a refugee camp near Vienna.

Even with this second pregnancy, I bled until I was four and a half months pregnant.

Out of mistrust, I did not go to a doctor until the baby started moving. Not speaking German well and being a refugee did excuse me from condemnation.

The Austrian and Canadian doctors were very kind to me. So, this child was okay, regardless of my immense struggles with health issues, infertility, medical accidents, etc. When I say medical accidents it is because the same doctor, Dr. Copil, who killed the first baby in me (my first pregnancy), was the very doctor who became my saviour angel, soon after. He saved me from having one of my ovaries removed. I can tell you that because of him I learned not to judge harshly anyone who commits a mistake. In time, I stopped grieving and started loving the child that God gave me. How do I know that it is not the same child/soul? I often wonder. Here I'd like to point out that Dr. Copil (gynecologist-specialist) from the city of Arad, was a totally different doctor than Dr. Copil (pediatrician-specialist) from the city of Bistrita. They were both very famous Romanian doctors with legions of people loving them, or ... some ... hating them. In my memoir I mentioned Dr. Copil from Bistrita as being the one who saved my life as a teenager.

About vacations in Romania, a few more things came to my mind that could be important. I realized that children, teenagers, university students, and seniors, are not being properly informed of how much fun they could have travelling there. We are talking quality, health, modernism, and blending of cultures.

Entertainment is everywhere! The food and drinks, I recall, are delicious and first class. Summer gardens, terraces, restaurants, elegant hotels, villas, bazaars, modern shopping centers, beauty competitions, nudism for those who prefer, tourism from around the world, etc.

The two things I will forever treasurer in my mind are: "The Marine Museum" in Constanta, and travelling with "The Tiny Train of Happiness" which is convertible.

Above all, I believe that the well mannered people that I encountered everywhere made my holidays so positively memorable. Clean, well mannered professionals who are naturally talented in customer service, create the best atmospheres for travelers. It is their way of living—tradition and professionalism is what they enjoy. They never get tired of being polite. It is in their blood.

Romanian people are sensitive by nature. For them playing hosts is not about money, it is about themselves, their capability to cure, to entertain, to serve, to impress with good and beauty—regardless of how tough their lives were through history.

History comes and goes, but what we present history with is, ourselves, the best of what we have, of who we are.

Hospitality, clean markets and department stores is what I experienced. Fresh bread and meat. Tasty milk and eggs. Natural honey and delicious cakes—and of course, I was pampered with home made food, special recipes found only in Romania.

People in Romania know how to cook!

They love to cook, both men and women. Even children get excited around the stove. It's fun! Like in the laboratory at school during chemistry class, only that instead of ammonia, you tamper with vanilla. With great sincerity, I suggest that everyone should go to Romania. While there, have a vanilla ice-cream, a glass of mineral water, a spritz, if you wish ... Cheers! = Salut!

The city of Bistrita—where I grew up from the age of two until the age of nineteen.

Student dancers—city of Cluj (or) Klausenburg, Transylvania, Romania. I received this post card on June 26, 1969 from a childhood friend, Teo, who went in the army (mandatory at the time). The image made me very happy. It reminded me of the time I traveled to Cluj to babysit my pediatrician's little boy while his wife went for her university exams. I loved Cluj and I went back there to visit quite a few times after. Sadly, Teo, my friend died of leukemia at the age of 22. He left behind a very young wife, his adorable baby boy, and this card.

Klausenburg is one of the seven great German cities built in Transylvania, as a fortress and commercial centre. This city has famous universities.

Chapter Three

CHILDREN'S INCREDIBLE

Talents

C hildren were very talented in Transylvania. Hard working little bees, adored by their parents, pampered by their grandparents, and rewarded for good behavior and their achievements in school. Respect for adults and for property was generally adopted. Community rules were respected. Fun was part of everyday life in my times as a child there, and so was physical activity. Hygiene was something that was verified at home and in school—from nails to everything else, including the uniform. Everyone was responsible: children, parents, teachers, etc. ... and times were good ... no crimes, no theft, no fear. Many of the children I went to school with ended up becoming famous. From Romania's Minister of Education to great sculptors, musicians, mayors, scientists, doctors, educators, economists, bankers, UN professionals (my own cousin), to award winning and best-selling authors, like me, etc.

Elderly people would whisper,

"There's something magnificent at work here. How can anyone explain this phenomena. It must be a secret blessing. It is in the mountains. It is in the air. It is in the prayer ... "

Only God knows what it was, but I can happily proclaim that I was born and grew up in a very blessed environment—free from worry, with wonderful people all around. What a wonderful childhood!

But times changed rapidly. The cloud of darkness started to suffocate the spirit of decent people.

Only as an adult, towards mid '70s, I started to discover and feel clearly "that great fear" that people were talking about.

... secrecy, conspiracy, and conspicuous eyes controlling the surroundings. I also believe that it had a lot to do with the city environment. In small towns and villages, people spoke openly about their feelings.

Peasants blasted the system day and night without too much fear. I guess that they did not realize, nor did they care.

The evil communist government escalated in its endeavours towards the '80s—then went overboard as they entered into the '90s. No wonder that everything came down crumbling. I can only imagine after I left, in 1980, what people went through until 1989 when the Revolution took place and president Ceausescu was executed.

ROMANIA CELEBRATES

Children

Romanian families always cared with great sensibility about the well being of their children and prepared way in advance for their future. Parents and grandparents invested everything they had in the little ones, with love and great hope.

I know, because I was born and I grew up there. Children were receptive and obedient. Most of them grew up loving their families to a great extreme. The love and respect for their parents was so great that many adult men and women would have tears in their eyes just looking at their parents or grandparents. (Do not get me wrong—there were sporadic exceptions).

History changed since I left. Millions

spread all around the world. Families were separated by distance. Many died on both sides without having the chance to even say goodbye. For many, the cruelty of separation became the ultimate poison.

The old saying that circulates around the globe suggesting that, "Only the strong will survive," is not quite accurate.

There are miracles, luck, and other factors that help us survive in the face of adversity. I'm proof of that. There is one thing I would agree with—that great distance becomes acceptable after a while. Again, being technologically inclined these days with Skype, computers, e-mails, smart phones ... the distance does not create such a big gap anymore. Like in the good old days, one family prepares the cake here in North America, the other family prepares the cake in Europe—then they sit together and experience a virtual birthday party, laughing, talking, crying, and so on.

From Romania, there are millions around the world. My own family is global. In the USA alone I have hundreds of family members, most I've never met. From New York, to Los Angeles, to Florida, etcetera ... I have family. And they are good Christian people. Most are conservative in their behavior and extremely successful in their professions. In Europe, many of my family members live in Germany, England, Austria, Ireland, Spain, Italy, Portugal, etc. Some are in Australia. Here, in Canada, I have quite a few. In fact, we have family in the US and Canada from before World War I, from which some went back, while others remained. The youngsters in my family living in Romania speak English, French, and German. One even learned Portuguese in university. I asked her, "Why?"

"I love it," she replied. A few started Latin in university ... and the list goes on. Romanians are very studious people. They love education. It makes me happy to see

that and I am very proud of my provenance.

The world, the countries have changed, and so did we. Gone are the days of small talk or small walk.

Now, in the modern 21st Century, we broadcast and we space travel.

We cannot hide our faces or our voices. Humanity is stripped of the old fashion costume of privacy. We better control our impulses. It is peace that we want! Prosperity! Smart travelling ... Global education ... Commerce ... Unity and agreement ... Peace ... and LOVE, under the umbrella of all the cosmic beauty that exists in reality, in our imagination, and in our dreams. We are children in It All.

From Canada, I send you love ... Here is paradise on Earth! What a privilege to be Canadian! It seems to me that I was double blessed in this life. I could only wonder about our immediate future ... the next places we'll colonize ... the new adventures we will be involved in ... new species we'll encounter ... the intelligence available at our disposal ...

***

Dear tourists and future parents,

Good trip to Romania!
I pray SOVATA and/or the other resorts will pro-
vide you with great fun—and help cure you, as it
helped me.
Preserve your faith and never listen to negative
people. I wish you success.

Dear Global Friends,

You are also invited to Canada!
Canada is very special—
and as rich as our imagination.
Canada is in the future already!
Paradise on Earth.

Welcome!

Elysse

My dear Global Friends

I, the experienced human, kindly ask you to please, note my suggestion:

Goggle the places that I mentioned in this book and you will find an incredible amount of up to date pictures, traveling tips, accommodations, etc. Customize your needs! Prepare a clear plan. Get opinions from variety of reliable sources. Trust is also necessary. Do not discount specialists and fertility clinics near you. (You know best).

Fertility Goddess SOVATA is my gift to those who are looking for extra information, and/or solutions. I wanted to write something that is helpful at many levels. The book also describes me, the author, in similar situations—times when I welcomed miracles and the help of professionals.

How lucky I was! ... to be cured. The fact that I encountered so many good souls on this planet makes me feel more than lucky. I feel special!

The lessons I learn in my journey?

Priceless ...

Good Luck

BIBLIOGRAPHY

Books written by Elysse Poetis™

* * *

THE MIND OF A POETESS

a true contemporary story
MEMOIR
for which Elysse received the
2007 Arts Acclaim Award.

I LOVE YOU

CANADIAN POETRY

FOREVER LOVED

LELU

written in the memory of Elysse's male cat, Lelu, who died unexpectedly (February 2010). Lelu's entire life, his love for Mitzy, and his death photographed by Elysse. Bestseller on Kindle.

THE NATURE OF BEAUTY

Canadian/Ontario Nature, Photography by Elysse

Fertility Goddess SOVATA

Discovery of possibility—Infertility can be cured

THE HUNTER OF BEAUTY

CANADA's architecture, Toronto, Ottawa, Waterloo, etc.
Artistic Photography by Elysse

GREAT FUN IN CANADA & USA

(soon to come)

Elysse resides in The Technology Triangle, Region of
Waterloo, Canada. She loves writing, photography, and
working with her husband/publisher on new concepts
and designs. Nature attracts her like a magnet, right into
its smallest detail.

www.elyssepoetis.com